TRUE BLUE

TRUE BLUE

*Living with Mental Illness in
the Shadow of the Steeple*

A glimpse into the mentally ill mind of a pastor's wife and
the struggle to clear the stigma surrounding her story. Facts,
statistics, and vulnerability combine to offer a clear explanation
of what the Christian community needs to know.

Pastor Tom
and
Tracy Monteith

WESTBOW˙
PRESS
A DIVISION OF THOMAS NELSON
& ZONDERVAN

WestBow Press books may be ordered through booksellers or by contacting:

WestBow Press
A Division of Thomas Nelson & Zondervan
1663 Liberty Drive
Bloomington, IN 47403
www.westbowpress.com
1 (866) 928-1240

ISBN: 978-1-4908-5178-5 (sc)

Library of Congress Control Number: 2014916372

Printed in the United States of America.

WestBow Press rev. date: 10/24/2014

"True Blue is a must read for every pastor, pastor's wife, executive pastor, family pastor or any Christian who lives with depression or mental illness. Most churches struggle with how to help those who do struggle. This book provides facts, research and practical steps to make the growing number of Christians struggling with mental illness feel acceptance and grace. This book is long overdue. It will change your church and your life."

Mitch Temple
Licensed Marriage-Family Therapist;
Former Director – Marriage, Focus
on the Family; Full-time Family
Pastor – 23 years; Consultant
for Faith and Family Films.

CONTENTS

ACKNOWLEDGEMENTS

First of all, we would like to acknowledge and praise our Lord and Savior, Jesus Christ, for planting the seed that inspired our hearts to write this book. Without Him, we can do nothing and we give God all the glory for any successes that this book might merit.

Secondly, we would like to thank our family: Mom for her constant encouragement to keep pressing on; Pops for his financial support; Micheil for his incredible editing skills and advice regarding grammatical correctness; Jonathan, Carly, Christopher, Jess, Kaitlyn and Michael for their love and support; and Caroline and Max for being a source of joy when we got discouraged.

We also want to acknowledge those that financially sponsored us with generous gifts: Kyle and Bethany, Eric and Debi, Joanna, Jeri, Kaitlyn, Tony and Becky. Without your sacrificial giving, the publishing of this work would not have been possible. Thank you!

God provided an unbelievable opportunity to work with a young, graphic designer who was willing to donate his time and talent. We want to introduce you to an amazing artist named Kenneth Crane. He spent countless hours designing the cover for this book and asked for nothing in return. Please take a moment to see more of his creative work at www.KennethCrane.com. Thank you, Kenny!

I have spent countless hours in therapy and counseling trying to manage this spot in my journey and without the help of my beloved husband, Karla, Scott, Jay and Becky, I would still be wandering.

Finally, our manuscript would not have made it this far without the inspiration of the following friends: Leon, Roy, Lisa, SarahBeth, Mitch, Aarin, Glenn, Joanna, Paula and Scott. You have all been such an encouragement to us and we thank the Lord upon every remembrance of you.

*"A personal testimony by those who have suffered has **double benefit**; we find meaning and purpose in our struggles if we can use them on behalf of others. At the same time, congregations learn that they do not have to be mental health experts to provide community support to families in crisis."* [1]

INTRODUCTION

This little girl sits happily on her pink polka-dotted bedspread, preparing to enter a land of fairy tale castles and white horses. She wants to enter into a dream land where she has the power to stop time and just lay in the soft, green grass, letting the gentle breeze kiss her cheek while she molds and shapes the clouds into lovely ocean scenery. A sense of calmness and total safety floods her mind. No one follows her there except her imaginary friends – friends that won't laugh at her, throw snowballs at her on the way home from school, or steal her lunch. No grown-ups are allowed there either. They have forgotten how to laugh and have fun, and are so wrapped up in things that don't matter that they can't see the necessity of deep breaths and clear, happy thoughts. She puts on her ballerina slippers and her plastic, jeweled crown. With great excitement she anticipates being transported to another world – a magical place where the prince will rescue her from every danger and disappointment. You see, he knows her heart and understands her fears. He understands the hurt she endures and will stop at nothing to cover the pain with comfortable, warm love, and genuine joy. He's the answer to all that confounds and troubles her. Nothing can penetrate the protective arms of her prince. She remains forever beautiful with long, flowing, brown locks, soft porcelain skin, and a princess ball gown that flows with her every move. She finally feels pretty and loveable, like she desperately longs to feel in the harsh world called 'reality'.

This kind of day-dreaming is expected out of a young girl, even an older teenager…but when a middle-aged, married woman lives in this world so much of the time that her reality becomes indistinguishable from her fantasy; then psychiatrists, therapists, family-members, and friends must step in to help pull her back from the ledge of confusion and insanity. She saturates the depths of her heart with unrealistic hopes and dreams until she starts to drown under the heavy waves of confliction and desperation. She can't see the rescuer's hands because her eyes are covered with scales of hopelessness. She only sees irrational answers of pills, razor blades, and ultimately death, as her way of escape.

The world of mental illness has many unique stories that all show a different aspect of the disease. This specific story is my own. The desperation and the dreaming, the fear and the fantasy, the confusion which is reality…they are all members of my mind. My reason for sharing the dark depths of my depression is simply to help, in some small way, another person who might be searching for that elusive strand of sanity – someone who, like me, lives one day at a time never knowing when the monster will rear its ugly head. Charles Haddon Spurgeon once said, *"Oh, that I might comfort some of my Master's servants. I have written out of my own heart with the view of comforting their hearts. I would say to them in their trials – My brethren, God is good. He will not forsake you; He will bear you through."* I want ministers, lay people, the mentally ill, and the community in general to be enlightened and educated so that ignorance and fear no longer exist. My desire is for ministers to have the courage and tools to help those in their flock who might be struggling in this area, for lay people in the church to confidently extend a loving hand to those they don't understand, for the mentally ill to learn to trust the church again, and for the general community to accept that not all illnesses are visible or easily understood. The apostle Paul very clearly said, the *"…God of all comfort…comforts us in all our tribulation, <u>that we may be able to comfort those</u> who are in any trouble, with the comfort with which we ourselves are comforted by God." (II Corinthians 1:3b-4).* Christ gives the perfect example of how to walk through difficulties. He shows us how to trust the Father, then use that hard time as comfort and encouragement for others just entering their own time of hardship. God works through our brokenness, from generation to generation. My prayer is that our story would point you back to the Author of our faith, the Lord Jesus Christ. He is the only One who can guide you through your own journey from brokenness to wholeness.

Chapter I

WHO AM I?

A Personal Look:

"Let me introduce myself. My name is Tracy and I play the piano. I play the piano a LOT! It's okay – I love to play. I play Brahms, Mozart, Rachmaninoff,… all the greats. I can easily lose myself in music when I sit down at the keyboard. I started taking lessons when I was three years old through a Yamaha course at the local church. I took to music like a duck to water! I thoroughly enjoy practicing for hours at a time in order to get a piece "just right". Practicing to perfection is a necessary evil and a way of life for me. My obsessive-compulsive perfectionism has actually helped in getting me into several local, state and regional competitions. I am playing at my church as well, and accompanying my junior high school choir. Music is like breathing to me.

I love it! So does my hamster! Peaches, the hamster, sits on my shoulder and listens to me play, pray, and drone on about school woes.

School is starting to stress me out a little bit though. Junior High is so different from elementary school! People who don't even know me tease and taunt me almost daily. I don't know why, because I work very hard at becoming one with the wallpaper. I don't talk in class unless the teacher insists I answer a question. I don't even make fun of the cheerleaders! I'm a good student – A's and a couple of B's in honors classes. I want to try out for the volleyball team, but my piano teacher won't let me. She says it would be too easy to jam a finger before an important competition. I guess she knows best, but the day she said "no" I shed a lot of tears … and again the next day … and the following weekend. I guess I tend to cry a lot; but not in public – just in my room or while I'm walking home from school every day by myself."

Looking back, I can recognize this time in my life as the beginning of changes in my personality. I considered myself extremely shy, very naïve, and rather tender to the things of God. I had accepted Christ as my personal Savior in 1974 at the age of seven. I remember our church having Vacation Bible School one week in July. I had the best time! The Pastor's wife was one of the leaders and she would always put her hands on my shoulders as I was working on a craft and tell me how Jesus must be smiling down on my work. I was drawn to her because of her tender touch of love and her words of encouragement and empowerment. I was very attentive to anything I could learn from her about the Christian faith. She always seemed so happy. I wondered if she ever experienced problems or disappointments. If she did (and I'm sure she did), no one would ever know it by her shining expression of joy. I wanted to be the "Mrs. Leonard" type of Christian. I continued to watch this Godly woman week after week and year after year. Her walk remained consistent. She truly was living out her faith.

As I grew and stumbled through Junior High, I started experiencing these huge mood swings. One day I would ace a science test, get the solo in band, and find a beautiful wildflower on my way home to hamburgers and ice cream. Things don't get much better than that! Twenty-four hours later, I would feel like I had fallen off a cliff. I would sit down for lunch in the cafeteria and someone would dump chocolate milk all over my sandwich. I would get spit wads stuck in my hair from a table of boys sitting behind me, laughing. On my walk home I would trip on a bump in the sidewalk and skin up my knees, ripping my jeans and getting pebbles stuck in my palms. It wasn't just a bad day; I would immediately feel like a total failure. It was impossible for me to counter-act those thoughts with the sunshine and smiles from the day prior. I would lie to my parents and tell them I was horribly sick so I could just stay home in bed instead of face what seemed like another impossible day. Of course, this could also be categorized as Junior High angst; complete with all its drama. Part-way through my 8th-grade year I created a hiding place in the back corner of my closet. It was just a spot behind a closed door where I could go and curl up on a bright pink beanbag chair, covered in an afghan my Grandma made just for me. I could hide from the world, cuddle multiple stuffed animals, and cry. My Shaun Cassidy poster was nailed to the wall beside me. Since boys didn't like me, I could at least wish that someday Shaun would see me. My private corner was quiet, dark, and personal. I could almost hear God speak to me there.

I've carried that idea of "running away and hiding" with me into my adult life; and even now, I journal about my dreams of being rescued from my lonely castle tower by a handsome prince. We escape the pains and struggles of this life and live happily ever after in a land far away. The fairy tale kingdom life eludes me, but God is slowly teaching me to be Kingdom-minded and reminds me that the Eternal Prince has already rescued me and is preparing a castle for me in a land far away!

> *"O LORD, You have searched me and known me. You know my sitting down and*

my rising up; You understand my thought afar off. You comprehend my path and my lying down, And are acquainted with all my ways. For there is not a word on my tongue, But behold, O LORD, You know it altogether. You have hedged me behind and before, And laid Your hand upon me. Such knowledge is too wonderful for me; It is high, I cannot attain it. Where can I go from Your Spirit? Or where can I flee from Your presence? If I ascend into heaven, You are there; If I make my bed in hell, behold, You are there. If I take the wings of the morning, And dwell in the uttermost parts of the sea, Even there Your hand shall lead me, And Your right hand shall hold me. If I say, "Surely the darkness shall fall on me," Even the night shall be light about me; Indeed, the darkness shall not hide from You, But the night shines as the day; The darkness and the light are both alike to You. For You formed my inward parts; You covered me in my mother's womb. I will praise You, for I am fearfully and wonderfully made; Marvelous are Your works, And that my soul knows very well. My frame was not hidden from You, When I was made in secret, And skillfully wrought in the lowest parts of the earth. Your eyes saw my substance, being yet unformed. And in Your book they all were written, The days fashioned for me, When as yet there were none of them. How precious also are Your thoughts to me, O God! How great is the sum of them! If I should count them, they would be more in number than the sand; When I awake, I am still with You. … Search me, O God, and know my heart; Try me, and know my anxieties; And see if there is any wicked way in me, And lead me in the way everlasting."

Psalm 139:1-18, 23, 24 NKJV

Just The Facts:

- Preschoolers are the fastest-growing market for anti-depressants. At least 4% of preschoolers – over 1 million – are clinically depressed.[2]

- 1 in 33 children and 1 in 8 adolescents suffer from depression.[3] This translates to over 2 million teens suffering from depression.[4]

- 70% of children do not receive treatment for their mental and emotional disorders.[3]

- Suicide is the 6th leading cause of death for 5 to 14 year olds. The number of attempted suicides is even higher.[5]

- 4% of preschoolers – over one million in number – are now clinically depressed and the rate of increase of depression among children is an astounding 23%.[6]

- There is a significant connection between artistic expression and mental illness.[7]

- The treatment success rate for a first episode of major depression is 65 – 70%.[8]

- 26.2% of Americans ages 18 and older suffer from a diagnosable mental disorder in a given year.[9]

- Depression is twice as common in women as it is in men.[10]

- 4 out of 5 runaway youths suffer from depression[11]

- A child can be diagnosed bi-polar as young as 6 years old[12]

- 100,000 individuals (most between 17 and 26 years) as a result of heredity and/or other factors that cause abnormal brain development become ill with schizophrenia each year[13]

- Four million children and adolescents in this country suffer from a *serious* mental disorder that causes significant functional impairments at home, at school and with peers. Of children ages 9 to 17, 21 percent have a diagnosable mental or addictive disorder that causes at least minimal impairment.[14]

- Half of all lifetime cases of mental disorders begin by age 14. Despite effective treatments, there are long delays, sometimes decades, between the first onset of symptoms and when people seek and receive treatment. An untreated mental disorder can lead to a more severe, more difficult to treat illness and to the development of co-occurring mental illnesses.[15]

- In any given year, only 20 percent of children with mental disorders are identified and receive mental health services.[16]

This should be more than enough information to understand how early in life mental illness can strike. If you have ten teens in your youth group at church, chances are that at least one of them is already struggling with mental illness in some form. Comments you hear about this child might include, "oh she's just very shy and socially awkward"; or "Jonny is just an angry little boy"; or even "what does his mother feed him? He's like Dr. Jekyll and Mr. Hyde!" Instead of passing judgment, why don't we as Christ-followers step back and ask ourselves if there just might be a deeper reason for their behavior? It could be that they are simply shy or socially awkward. Or it could be any number of other disorders that are treatable when caught early. Raising a child does require, in some aspects, an entire community. Why can't we extend our prayer support and help to other parents? Hopefully the contents of this book will equip you to accomplish that.

A Pastoral Look:

My initial encounter with Tracy was while we were still making our way through the emotional maze that high school often becomes. I was a transfer student from Bellevue, Nebraska; and she was a Colorado Springs, Colorado native. I was a sports fanatic and varsity athlete; she was a quiet, unassuming musician. Our paths only crossed because her best friend wanted to meet me and put Tracy up to arranging a date. Instead of agreeing to the proposed arrangement, I went out on that date with Tracy! From our very first meeting I knew that there was something different about her. I couldn't quite put my finger on it, but I could just tell that she was not like any other girl that I had ever shown an interest in during my youth. She was mysteriously intriguing. She was a Christian. I was not a Christian and only darkened the door of a church on Christmas and Easter. God definitely brought us together and Tracy was very instrumental in me coming to Christ; through her actions, words, and testimony of God's grace. Not once during our courtship did mental health ever come up as a concern. We both felt very comfortable and "normal" in our relationship; but things are not always what they seem.

I was so blind to the early signs of depression in Tracy's life. The family members that I had that struggled with mental illness were adults who had struggled with their condition for years. Although I loved learning and took all sorts of classes, there was nothing that taught me as a young man what to look for. Looking back, I wonder how I missed it. The warning signs were all there. Tracy was so incredibly timid when I first met her that I thought that her shyness was extremely cute. I remember one day, after watching her from afar, deciding to make my first move to speak with this adorable girl. She was playing piano in the choir room during a vocal practice for the spring musical so I walked up and slid onto the edge of the piano bench where she was sitting quietly. When I started to make small talk in my pathetic attempt to appear cool, she slid away from me, dropped her head, and would only respond in whispers without making any eye contact.

Well, this was an unexpected response to my advances! However, I thought it was just because she was so demure, a quality that I found refreshing. It wasn't until years later that I found out that she acted that way out of fear that I was just teasing her or that I was setting her up for the treatment that she had suffered from for years from guys "like me." She was in her early stages of depression and had learned to withdraw from peers as a protective reflex.

When Tracy and I started actually dating I was so excited to find out that under that coy shell was an intelligent, kind, and beautiful young lady. She showed me by her standards and values what it meant to be a Christian, a testimony that eventually helped me get to the point where I received the love of God in my life and surrendered to Jesus Christ as my Lord and Savior. We were connecting but I always felt like she was only giving me glimpses into who she really was. There is a proverb of Latin origin that states that "still waters run deep." I finally understood what that truly meant – this girl I was falling in love with had a certain duality; the Tracy everyone saw, and the true Tracy who was confused and scared by what she struggled with day after day. Every time I would get close to that part of Tracy, she would default back to her learned behavior of self-protection.

Chapter II

WHAT'S HAPPENING TO ME?

A Personal Look:

By High School I learned how to build a wall of protection around my heart and my life. It became easier to blend in, and I could always hide in the choir room or the band room without fear of someone whispering behind my back or knocking my books down the stairs. I learned which classes I had to get to early in order to get the desk in the back corner. I became adept at knowing which hallway provided safe passage between Chemistry and History class. I gave a valiant attempt at avoiding the verbal harassment from Polly (captain of the belittling brigade) and her groupies, but her vicious tongue played an effective role in crumbling my fragile self-esteem.

"It's now my senior year and God has dropped my prince right out of heaven and into my life. We are engaged to be married in June! Because he is a football player, the popular group (also known as my primary source of stress) leaves me alone now. Just his presence is protection for me from the outside world of hypocrisy and judgment. I've always felt so weak, but Tom is so strong. I've always "just played the piano", but he says I have a gift and a talent and loves to hear me play. He is the answer to all my problems and fears! He makes me feel accepted, cherished, and beautiful – all things I have never believed about myself. After the wedding we are moving to the Chicago area where Tom will be attending Naval Machinist Mate 'A' School. I can't wait to finally start the happy and perfect life I have always dreamed about!"

We were almost 19 years old and had the whole world in front of us. We rented a cute little efficiency apartment in Waukegan, Illinois, and furnished it with cardboard boxes and foam furniture. Life was good…sometimes. Tom would go to work, and I would watch soap operas and walk the dog. (Ironically, our cocker spaniel's name was 'Princess' – completing the fairy tale theme of my warped view on life.) When Tom would come home from work, we would share a wonderfully romantic meal of mac & cheese and tuna fish, followed by warm lemon cake for dessert. We would go to the park on his days off and play football in the leaves, or swing on the swings. We were so in love!

Oddly enough, I began feeling very alone…even in the midst of crowds of people. Have you ever sat back and compared yourself to all the other "normal" people in the world and wondered what was wrong with you? I quickly realized that I struggled with things that seemed so simple to other people. The more alone I felt, the more I would obsess over things I had control over. Things like my daily routine, the menu, and which kitchen drawer the utensils went in suddenly became extremely important to me. I thought if I could just make those things perfect, then Tom would love me even more! I would try to hang on to these little things, but something seemed to always spoil my plans. Tuesdays were the appointed time to walk the mall and window shop, and Tom was supposed to be home by 6:00. If he called to tell me the Master Chief was requiring him to stay for mandatory study time 'til 8:00, I would completely lose control. Something as simple as Thursday night's dinner being changed from hamburgers to stew would totally unravel me. Changing things, especially at the last minute, always threw me into a battle in my own mind. The logical side would say that dinner was still being put on the table so it didn't matter if the menu changed slightly; then the emotional side would argue back with what a waste it was to have bought the hamburger buns fresh if we weren't going to use them that night. That mental banter would almost consume my thinking! I would lose my ability to see the big picture and be stuck in a sea of insignificant details. I also started noticing that I obsessed over things that didn't seem to matter to anyone else! If the apartment wasn't spotless at the end of the day, I couldn't sleep at night. Self-deprecation became a daily habit that would escalate to poisonous levels. Something was wrong with me. The more I would try to hang on to things, the quicker they would slip out of my grip like sand through my fingers. I found myself screaming and crying uncontrollably when Tom went to work. "Why am I doing this?" I would ask. There was no reason for the outrageous behavior. No one was with me in our little apartment, so my fits weren't for show. Tom and I hadn't been fighting (yet!), so anger didn't spark my ranting. It wasn't always about anything specific, so why the need to cry for hours at a time? I am a curious creature by nature, so I started seeking information. Google was not yet on the scene, so I actually had to go to the library and start digging for helpful information in the pages of textbooks and medical journals. It was a tedious task, and I soon tired of searching for something I couldn't explain. My husband was the band-aid on my hurt. When he came home, the clouds parted, the rainbow appeared, and the flowers would dance on the doorstep of my day. This Jekyll-and-Hyde behavior continued for several years. Crying out for help was not an option! Navy wives were not weak, and our husbands had no time for petty little problems. After all, they were defending our country, risking their lives for our well-being. I needed to just put my big girl panties on and deal with it! I began journaling a lot at this point – expressing my irrational issues thru pen and paper. Little did I know at the time, but I was experiencing the effects of undiagnosed, untreated mental illness. It would not get better, it would get much worse. I was spiraling downward, and my outlook was getting darker and darker. I could still put on my game face around others, but the battle going on in my mind when I was by myself was quickly becoming a giant that I could not possibly defeat by myself!

> *"For my sighing comes before I eat, and my groaning pours out like water. For the thing I greatly feared has come upon me, and what I dreaded has happened to me. I am not at ease, nor am I quiet; I have no rest, for trouble comes."*
>
> *Job 3:24-26*

Just The Facts:

- Definition of mental illness: "any of various disorders characterized chiefly by abnormal behavior or an inability to function socially, including diseases of the mind and personality and certain diseases of the brain. Also called *mental disease, mental disorder.*"[17]

- Another definition of mental illness: "a group of brain disorders that cause severe disturbances in thinking, feeling, and relating, often resulting in an inability to cope with the ordinary demands of life."[18]

- In general, signs and symptoms may indicate a mental illness when they make you miserable and interfere with your ability to function in your daily life. You may have trouble coping with stress, anger or other emotions. Or you may find it difficult to handle family, work or school responsibilities, or have serious legal or financial problems.[19]

- Shame, fear, denial, and other factors often prevent individuals or their families from seeking help.[20]

- About 11.4 million adult Americans suffered from severe mental illness in the past year and 8.7 million adults contemplated serious thoughts of suicide. Among them, more than 2 million made suicide plans and about 1 million attempted suicide.[21]

- Two million Americans have schizophrenia disorders, and 300,000 new cases are diagnosed each year.[22]

A Pastoral Look:

After a romantic courtship and eventual marriage, I began to notice some peculiarities in my beautiful bride. She seemed to throw herself so hard into every endeavor that she would wear herself out. She also seemed to me (with no education in the field) as suffering from perfectionism, bordering on Obsessive-Compulsive Disorder. Everything she did had to be perfect, and her mood would darken considerably when things did not turn out well or meet her high standards. She never seemed to do anything for relaxation, but it almost seemed as if she was trying to discover who she was by attempting all of these "projects". When Tracy and I exchanged our vows at such a young age, I wonder how much of that part of the vows that said "in sickness and in health" I truly understood. I think that I was ready for some of the possible curve balls life would throw at us such as cancer, heart disease, and high blood pressure, because of the family histories; however, I was not prepared for what would come next.

This, of course, was before her diagnosis of mental illness and it seemed everything I tried did not work. People suffering from serious depression often struggle with identity and self-worth issues. Without knowing how Tracy processed information, I went about "helping" with no success. The harder I tried, the more Tracy expressed to me that she thought she was a failure – that she couldn't do anything right and that no one needed her. It is shocking how clueless I was at the time to these classic warning signs. As the situation worsened, I noticed that her spiritual life began to be affected by her depression. Just as Job's friends, with possible good intentions, pointed to him as the root cause of all his problems; many of our Christian brothers and sisters in the church started giving their own unsolicited advice. Some would tell her she just needed to pray more, have more faith, and some had the insensitivity to say she should just snap out of it. The real problem started when Tracy approached church leadership. She was summarily dismissed by some and told by others it was a demonic oppression and only Jesus could help her. It became painfully obvious to me that there was a serious problem in the church that stemmed from ignorance.

The evidence from my own experience is clear – there are many people in our churches asking the same question Tracy struggled with: "What is happening to me?"

Chapter III

IS DEPRESSION REAL?

A Personal Look:

"What is going on with me? How can I get someone…anyone, to understand what I'm going through? I can't get myself out of bed in the morning. I have no motivation to do anything. My babies no longer bring me joy. Hours go by without me accomplishing anything but turning the television on; and once it's on, I have no idea what I've watched. Some days I get around to brushing my teeth, some days I don't. I'm so tired all the time, and the mystery pain does not let up. Why is God doing this to me? Why can't I get any answers? Even my so-called friends have stopped coming by. What is wrong with me?"

At this point in our young family's life, Tom was out of the Navy and, quite frankly, burned out. He was working a full-time job at a juvenile detention facility, a part-time job making pizzas, and putting in several hours a week at church. I was a stay-at-home working mom for our four children under the age of eight. My life was very heavy; full of stagnation and clouds. Why wasn't it just "going away"? I deeply loved my kids and felt it was a privilege to stay home and teach them. I wanted to go out and socialize, even if it just meant going to church, but it was so challenging and draining. People started pulling away from me. They understandably didn't want my gloomy mood to rub off on them. Soon even my husband doubted that there was anything really wrong with me, besides a bad attitude. He told me I needed to rely on the scriptures more. He recommended the book of Psalms. "Read the Bible more? That's your advice? It's a struggle to even get clothes on in the morning. I need my 7-year-old son to pour cereal for his two younger brothers. It's a challenge to brush my hair; and you say, 'read your Bible more'?" I'm frustrated with my husband for not understanding me and fixing my problem. Maybe HE'S the one with the problem! After all, he used to be the answer to all my questions; the cherry on my sundae; the harmony to my melody. Now he's just another uncaring person who happens to live in my house. Where did my Prince Charming go? It was time for a change. We decided to move to Colorado and find a church where we could serve full time. I think both of us were hoping that a change in scenery would make my little cloud of gloom dissipate. God provided the 'perfect' opportunity for us – a church and school that wanted to hire both of us and allow our children to experience a private, Christian education. What could be better? In addition to teaching upper level sciences and Bible classes in the high school, Tom was preaching, coaching football, and building a youth department. I was teaching munchkins (also known as 4-year-olds), eating lunches with my children, helping Tom with the teenagers, and absolutely loving it. Being overly busy became my new method of handling 'the things I couldn't explain'. It was working! My new addiction to busyness shrouded the ugly, real me and the only cost I could find was exhaustion. That seemed like a worthwhile trade-off. After all, I could simply go home and collapse into bed and let the rest of life just happen without me for a few hours while I escaped to my castle. The 900 square feet we called home was nothing but cold walls that reflected that horrible place called 'reality'. My dream-land was much more appealing.

Tom, by now, is exasperated with me for not pushing through this period of doubt in my Christian walk. After several visits to the doctor, x-rays, lab-work, and tests - the results were in. Honestly, I was expecting Dr. Jeff to tell me I was dying. "Tracy, I believe you have depression" were his words. He had to be joking!

Did he mix up my file with someone else's? There's no way that could be true. He went on… "I want you to try a medication that should help the fatigue and moodiness." "NO!!" I screamed. I started crying uncontrollably. "You're wrong! Why can't you figure out what's wrong with me? I'm not just sad! I have pain and confusion and anger! I can't sleep! I'm not crazy, there's something PHYSICALLY wrong with me!" I ran out of the office, through the parking lot, and locked myself in my car. I cried from the dark depths of my broken soul and begged God to have mercy on me. My body was shaking and writhing in pain. I couldn't go on like this - not one more day. After about 45 minutes of sobbing, I started home to give Tom the bad news: the doctor failed to find any answers and I was doomed to live like this forever. We had a discussion after dinner and I told him what had transpired at the doctor's office.

That night, as I tried to drift off to sleep, the immenseness of the day filled my head. 'So what is depression? What does 'mental illness' really mean? What if it's not even real?!' All of these questions were swirling around in my mind as I tried to determine what was happening to me. My perception was one of consuming fear and utter confusion around this one question: **Is this real?** Maybe my perception isn't truth. It had to be a figment of my imagination that decided to plant itself in my brain and take root. I was a weak, misunderstood shell

of what a Christian woman should be. My thoughts took control and for the first time I questioned if suicide was the answer. My children would certainly be better off without me. Tom could find a better wife - a whole, healthy and beautiful wife. I'm dragging him down. …
What was I saying?

After many days of coercing, I finally agreed to try the medication. What could it hurt? I was dying anyway, so taking a pill each morning wasn't going to change that. I would indulge Dr. Jeff and my husband. That day was the start of a new, incredible journey of learning for me. I discovered that depression IS a very real and crippling disease; as are the countless other maladies that are classified under the stigmatic label which is Mental Illness.

The National Institute of Mental Health describes the physiology of mental illness best in the article 'Information about Mental Illness and the Brain':

"The term mental illness clearly indicates that there is a problem with the mind. But is it just the mind in an abstract sense, or is there a physical basis to mental illness? As scientists continue to investigate mental illnesses and their causes, they learn more and more about how the biological processes that make the brain work are changed when a person has a mental illness. Before thinking about the problems that occur in the brain when someone has a mental illness, it is helpful to think about how the brain functions normally. The brain is an incredibly complex organ. It makes up only 2 percent of our body weight, but it consumes 20 percent of the oxygen we breathe and 20 percent of the energy we take in. It controls virtually everything we as humans experience, including movement, sensing our environment, regulating our involuntary body processes such as breathing, and controlling our emotions. Hundreds of thousands of chemical reactions occur every second in the brain; those reactions underlie the thoughts, actions, and behaviors with which we respond to environmental stimuli. In short, the brain dictates the internal processes and behaviors that allow us to survive.

How does the brain take in all this information, process it, and cause a response? The basic functional unit of the brain is the **neuron**. A neuron is a specialized cell that can produce different actions because of its precise connections with other neurons, sensory receptors, and muscle cells. A typical neuron has four structurally and functionally defined regions: the cell body, **dendrites**, **axons**, and the axon terminals.

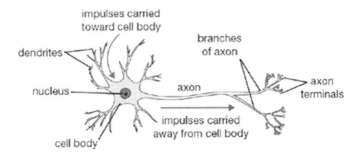

Near its end, the axon divides into many fine branches that have specialized swellings called axon terminals or pre-synaptic terminals. The axon terminals end near the dendrites of another neuron. The dendrites of one neuron receive the message sent from the axon terminals of another neuron.

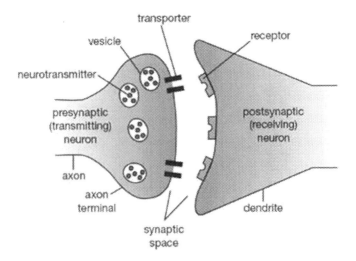

The site where an axon terminal ends near a receiving dendrite is called the **synapse**. It has been estimated that there are more synapses in the human brain than there are stars in our galaxy. Furthermore, synaptic connections are not static. Neurons form new synapses or strengthen synaptic connections in response to life experiences. This dynamic change in neuronal connections is the basis of learning.

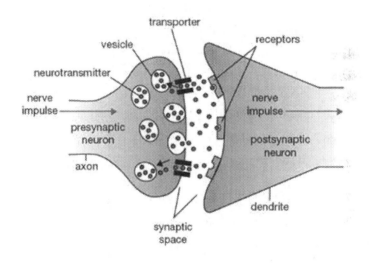

Neurons communicate using both electrical signals and chemical messages. Information in the form of an electrical impulse is carried away from the neuron's cell body along the axon of the pre-synaptic neuron toward the axon terminals. When the electrical signal reaches the pre-synaptic axon terminal, it cannot cross the synaptic space, or synaptic cleft. Instead, the electrical signal triggers chemical changes that can cross the synapse to affect the postsynaptic cell. After the neurotransmitter stimulates an electrical impulse in the postsynaptic neuron, it releases from the receptor back into the synaptic space. Specific proteins called **transporters** or **reuptake pumps** carry the neurotransmitter back into the pre-synaptic neuron. When the neurotransmitter molecules are back in the pre-synaptic axon terminal, they can be repackaged into vesicles for release the next time an electrical impulse reaches the axon terminal. Enzymes present in the synaptic space degrade neurotransmitter molecules that are not taken back up into the pre-synaptic neuron.

The nervous system uses a variety of neurotransmitter molecules, but each neuron specializes in the synthesis and secretion of a single type of neurotransmitter. Some of the predominant neurotransmitters in the brain include glutamate, GABA, **serotonin**, dopamine, and norepinephrine. Each of these neurotransmitters has a specific distribution and function in the brain; the specifics of each are beyond the scope of this module, but a few of the names will arise in reference to particular mental illnesses."[23]

With so many intricacies in the brain; many of which science still doesn't completely understand; even a small glitch in the networking can throw off the delicate chemical balance resulting in any number of mental problems.

Just The Facts:

- An estimated 26.2 percent of Americans ages 18 and older — about one in four adults — suffer from a diagnosable mental disorder in a given year.[24]

- MRIs and PET scans have shown differences in brain structure, mass and function in schizophrenics.[25]

- Major Depressive Disorder is the leading cause of disability in the U.S. for ages 15-44.[26]

- People don't always know what to say to someone who's battling depression. Here are 10 helpful things to say that show you care:

    1. You're not alone in this.
    2. You are important to me.
    3. Do you want a hug?
    4. You are not going crazy.
    5. We are not on this earth to see through one another, but to see one another through.
    6. When all this is over, I'll still be here and so will you.
    7. I can't really understand what you are feeling, but I can offer my compassion.

8. I'm not going to leave you or abandon you.
9. I care about you.
10. I'm sorry that you're in so much pain. I am going to take care of myself, so you don't need to worry that your pain might hurt me.

Conversely, here are 10 things NOT to say to someone dealing with depression:

1. There's always someone worse off than you are.
2. No one ever said that life was fair.
3. Stop feeling sorry for yourself.
4. So you're depressed. Aren't you always?
5. Try not to be so sad.
6. It's your own fault.
7. Believe me, I know how you feel. I was depressed once for several days.
8. I think your depression is a way of punishing us.
9. Haven't you grown tired of all this "me, me, me" stuff yet?
10. Have you tried chamomile tea?[27]

• As scientists continue to investigate the brains of people who have mental illnesses, they are learning that mental illness is associated with changes in the brain's structure, chemistry, and function and that mental illness does indeed have a biological basis.[28]

Save me, O God! For the waters have come up to my neck. [2] I sink in deep mire, Where there is no standing; I have come into deep waters, Where the floods overflow me.

Psalm 69:1-2

[9] *And He said to me, "My grace is sufficient for you, for My strength is made perfect in weakness." Therefore most gladly I will rather boast in my infirmities, that the power of Christ may rest upon me. [10] Therefore I take pleasure in infirmities, in reproaches, in needs, in persecutions, in distresses, for Christ's sake. For when I am weak, then I am strong.*

2 Corinthians 12:9 – 10

A Pastoral Look:

When Tracy finally received a diagnosis, I was introduced to terms and definitions that were previously confined to other people's lives: depression, panic attacks, psychosis, and suicidal ideations. "Didn't these things only happen to non-Christian families? How could God allow such a thing to happen to my wife? Didn't He know that I was not able to bear this burden?" These were only a few examples of the plethora of questions that raced through my mind. My emotions were just as varied; alternating between anger, confusion, discouragement, worry, bitterness, and even denial. None of these things could change the veracity of what was happening to the love of my life. Tracy was diagnosed with severe clinical depression. Our lives would be forever altered by this diagnosis.

I need to be clear about the source of my reaction to the news. I was, at the time, a young preacher who had been listening to other preachers (many of whom were my mentors) spout their own personal beliefs on the subject of mental illness. Their vocalizations were fueled by ignorance, prejudice, and I believe, fear. That was my problem. I was not able to separate their opinions from God's Word. I assumed if they proclaimed it from the pulpit, it must obviously be from God! I was devastated when I realized that some ministers teach their own beliefs and convictions as if they were directly from God. Because of my lack of discernment, I allowed their dogma to guide my response. I doubted the validity of Tracy's condition. After all, Christians could not possibly be mentally ill, could they? Mental illness was only a manifestation of demonic influence, wasn't it? Maybe mental illness wasn't even a real condition. It's only for those too weak to just "get over it", right? None of these reservations could change this new path we were beginning to journey down as a couple. This was happening. This was, and continues to be, very real.

During my years of counseling I have had many come to me with apparent symptoms of mental illness. Allow me to insert a personal opinion here – if you are a pastor, you are a Bible and life counselor. Know where your limitations are. I have a list of Christian licensed therapists, psychologists, and psychiatrists close at hand that I refer congregants to. It is also a good idea to recommend they see a medical doctor as well because depression may be the result of a serious medical condition.

Here are just a few examples I have personally witnessed (names have been changed):

- Janet, who is an integral part of many church ministries, has been struggling with the mounting pressure of raising children. Her husband has always believed that the extent of his role in the family is to earn money for the household. This has led Janet to feel isolated, worn out, and discouraged. That in itself seems to be fairly common; however, Janet has been struggling with hearing voices her entire life, even after receiving Christ. These voices began to get worse, telling her to run away and abandon her family, and at other times attempting to coerce her to harm herself.

- Joe is a Sunday School teacher that truly loves the Lord. He is a family man and is known for his outgoing personality. Joe has seemed to remain strong regardless of what circumstances come his way. His wife unfortunately sees a lot of warning signs behind the scenes and asked him to come and speak with me about a few issues. During the course of our talks, it comes out that he has a strong addictive personality. Those closest to him were unaware that he is addicted to drugs, pornography, and illicit affairs. He was so deeply traumatized by things in his past that he is trying to cover his hurt with addictions. Joe continues to see a professional.

- A pastor's wife (we will call her Susan) always seemed to be a little eccentric to those her husband was called to shepherd. She was raised in a Christian home by a fairly well known preacher in the Bible Belt. Her behavior became more and more erratic. She would have moments of what can almost be called "giddiness" but on other days she would be volatile, with violent behavior becoming more commonplace. Her behavior worsened and she continued to resist getting help. She began to try to harm her husband while he was sleeping and throwing objects at him for no reason. She ended up running away, getting a divorce, and basically disappearing from all who knew her.

- Beth was a deacon's wife. She had lived most of her life with self-loathing and moments of severe depression. This was compounded by how she perceived the qualifications of a deacon's wife in the scripture. She felt she was unable to meet the impossible standard she had set for herself which caused her to spiral further and further into her depression, causing her to struggle to even get out of her bed.

- A preacher named George is known for a warm personality and being quick to laugh. He began experiencing pain, insomnia, stomach issues and panic attacks. He became very hard to live with. One of his issues is that he is one of those Christians that was taught that if someone was depressed it just meant they weren't praying enough. He finally sought professional help and is in recovery.

- A deacon's sister has a history of multiple risky sexual encounters that she has been using to cover how she truly felt. Her self-image issues and depression were key factors in her behavior.

When asked, she will respond that she knows it is sin and that she is tearing apart her family. However, she is feeling incapable of coping with it. She has sought help from churches and was told she just needed to pray more.

- I had one man in my office that I have great respect for – hard working, confident, a "manly man" if you will. He is a hulking man that loves to work with his hands, fish and hunt. Sitting across from me he began to weep. Not just tear up, his large frame was wracked with sobs. He didn't want to do anything anymore – didn't want to work, didn't want to enjoy leisure activities, didn't even want to get out of bed. The issue? He has been covering up severe depression for so long that he reached a breaking point. Praise God he is getting the help he needs.

I could give many more examples, but these are just a few examples of what one preacher has experienced. Instead of ignoring the problem, we need to be the conduit of the power and grace of God in these hurting people's lives!

Now I want to address a rather controversial topic: demonic possession. The church historically has one of two reactions to the subject of mental illness to which I already alluded. The first has been to automatically see mental illness as an incident of demonic possession. The second has been to essentially ignore the issue - an "ostrich head in the sand" approach. Let us examine the dangers of the first of these responses (the other response will be dealt with in a later chapter).

I believe in the scriptural reality of demonic possession. The apostle Paul warns us that *"we do not wrestle against flesh and blood, but against principalities, against powers, against the rulers of the darkness of this age, against spiritual hosts of wickedness in the heavenly places."* **(Ephesians 6:12 NKJV).** Demonic activity is not only real, it is the source of our daily battles! It would be so much easier for all of us if we could see or touch our enemy; however, our enemy is cunning and deceitful, laying in wait for Christians. *"Be sober; be vigilant; because your adversary the devil walks about like a roaring lion, seeking whom he may devour."* **(1 Peter 5:8 NKJV)**

The first problem with the church reacting by ascribing all mental illness symptoms to demonic possession is that (based on God's Word) a true blood-washed, born again believer cannot be possessed. When we receive Jesus Christ we are given the gift of the indwelling of the Holy Spirit by God's wonderful grace. As Jesus was teaching his disciples, he reveals this blessed promise in **John 14:16-17**: *"And I will pray the Father, and He will give you another Helper, that He may abide*

***with you forever— the Spirit of truth, whom the
world cannot receive, because it neither sees Him
nor knows Him; but you know Him, for He dwells
with you and will be in you.*** " The Spirit's indwelling
has many purposes in our lives – conviction, guidance,
teaching, and reproof, to name a few. Although the
activities of God the Holy Spirit are diverse, the one
commonality is that if He is in us, demons cannot
be! In **2 Corinthians 6:14** Paul questions the church
by asking them, ***"what communion has light with
darkness?"*** God, as the true light, indwelling the
believer, will not have communion with the demonic
forces which are darkness. Therefore, a pastor or church
that dismisses the mentally ill as demonically possessed
are saying that anyone suffering from mental illness is
not spiritually saved.

Another problem with assuming every mentally ill
person is suffering at the hands of demons is that it
ignores the scriptural examples of what may very well
be symptomatic of depression and other mental illness.
I am not a psychologist, but it appears to me that some
of these cases point to recognizable warning signs of
depression or other mental illness.

- Jonah - He began to despair and sink into what
  may have been depression and thoughts of dying
  after God saved the people of Nineveh. Notice
  his cry to the Lord in **Jonah 4:3** *"Therefore*

now, O LORD, please take my life from me, for it is better for me to die than to live!"

- Job - Job arguably suffered more than most Bible personalities. After losing his livestock, his children, and his health, he was a broken man. Read Job's own words in **Job 6:1-3** and **8-10**: ***"Then Job answered and said: "Oh, that my grief were fully weighed, And my calamity laid with it on the scales! For then it would be heavier than the sand of the sea— Therefore my words have been rash." … "Oh, that I might have my request, That God would grant me the thing that I long for! That it would please God to crush me, That He would loose His hand and cut me off! Then I would still have comfort; Though in anguish I would exult, He will not spare; For I have not concealed the words of the Holy One."***

- Elijah - We cannot doubt the intensity and passion of this incredible man of God. This is the prophet that faced down the servants of the pagan false god of Baal on Mount Carmel, calling down fire by the power of the one and only true God! Yet Elijah finds himself facing an emotional crisis, maybe depression, under a juniper tree where God, in his mercy and grace, supplies his needs. Later, while fleeing from the wicked Jezebel, his discouragement leads him to hiding in a cave. God responds to Elijah's condition by asking what he was doing in a cave, to which he replied in **1 Kings 19:14**, *"I have been very zealous for the LORD God of hosts; because the children of Israel have forsaken Your covenant, torn down Your altars, and killed Your prophets with the sword. I alone am left; and they seek to take my life."*

- David - David was a man who had an extremely difficult life – much of which he brought on himself through his own sin. The Psalms are literally filled with examples of David's struggle with symptoms of mental illness but we will only reference two of them: *"I am troubled, I am bowed down greatly; I go mourning all the day long. …I groan because of the turmoil of my heart"* (Psalm 38:6, 8). *"When I kept silent, my bones grew old Through my groaning all the day long. For day and night Your hand was heavy upon me; My vitality was turned into the drought of summer. Selah."* (Psalm 32:3-4)

Do we then dismiss the symptoms of these mentioned above as demonic possession? Absolutely not! We must understand the reality of mental illness. It is an illness afflicting many ... possibly someone that may be sitting next to you in the pew. It is as real as cancer, diabetes, and heart disease.

Chapter IV

WHERE DID MY FRIENDS & FAMILY GO?

A Personal Look:

"Honey, I need to run back up to the church for about an hour. I forgot to copy practice pages for my kindergarteners for tomorrow morning. We always practice printing our letters on Thursdays. I'm so excited with their progress! Whoever said 4-yr. olds weren't capable of reading or writing needs to come visit my class! Would you mind getting the kids ready for bed? I can give Kate a bath in the morning if you can bathe the boys tonight while I'm gone."

It's really cold tonight! After a long day at school in a stuffy room with 28 ankle-biters, followed by an evening of teaching teenagers, the brisk air outside is a welcome change in the atmosphere. I take my time starting up the van and turn the radio off. Silence. Heavy sigh. Cleansing breath. Much better. I am so blessed to have a husband that doesn't mind being a daddy after a long day at work. I close my eyes to offer up a quick prayer of thanks for Tom and my children, and then turn the radio back on. I back the van out of the driveway and make my way down the street a few short blocks to the church and school where we are employed. The building is locked up and dark following Wednesday night services. I park in the side lot, closest to my classroom, then walk around to the front door and enter my code to turn the alarm off. The building is so quiet at night – a stark contrast to the hustle and bustle of 200 students crowding the hallways during the day. I quickly walk upstairs, turning lights on as I go, and get the copier warming up while I go back downstairs to my classroom to grab my lesson plans. Autumn leaves made out of construction paper line the doorframe while drawings of God's creatures hang from the ceiling of the little classroom. Splashes of creativity and giggles of innocence are frequent visitors within these friendly walls. I climb the stairs again and make the necessary copies for tomorrow's lessons and re-trace my steps, turning things off. I head toward the side door to exit and go home. I'm looking forward to my warm bed and a good night's sleep!

As I get into the van and crank the engine, I notice the three suspicious shadows on the playground. I open the driver side door and stand, yelling, "Hey there! You guys need to clear off the property. This is a church and school and I'd rather you not be smoking here." They turn and look. The shorter one puts out his cigarette, then they look at each other, mumbling under their breath. "Go on home now." Teenage boys… They need to be in our youth department instead of….. They are certainly in a hurry to… "Stop! … No! …" I push the open door towards him and try to get in the van, but not before his left fist hits my face. As my head snaps back and hits the metal doorframe, the dark engulfs me.

I don't recall how much time passes – but my ears open first to the dinging of the open door of my running vehicle. In the cold blackness I hear muffled voices and foul language. My nostrils get a strong whiff of alcohol and sweat. My eyelids cautiously open and my blank stare is fixed on two blinking red dots, blinking in perfect rhythm. Blink – blink – ding, ding, ding. The soft edges of unconsciousness curl back to reveal the piercing pain of reality as I begin to understand what is happening. "Tom", I quietly whisper. Slap! "Shut up!" he yells. I feel a single tear ever-so-slowly finding its way over the bridge of my nose, under my other eye, and then down my cheek to its resting place on the passenger seat of the van. Shots of pain keep grinding into my back. The emergency brake between the seats would dig deeper every time my body was pressed upon by his movements. Then a groan and his hands pushed hard on my chest. Why couldn't I move? Am I paralyzed? This is just a nightmare. "Tom… please…", I cried. The second young boy assumes his position and begins the torture all over again. My ears block the sounds of their laughter. My nose becomes dull to the stench of beer and cheap cologne. I close my eyes, firmly believing this is what death feels like; but the blinking dots of the digital clock keep beating on my eyelids not allowing me to succumb. I am falling….spinning…..tumbling in darkness. "Please God, where are You?" To my faithless surprise, He answers immediately! "My child, I'm right here with you."

I share the painful story of my rape in order to illuminate what trauma can do to someone who is already experiencing the effects of mental illness. Post-Traumatic Stress Disorder is most often linked to military men and women who have served in combat during a time of war; but can be a diagnosis for anyone who has gone through a severe traumatic experience. What I have learned is that trauma is defined as uniquely as the individual who experiences it. Witnessing a car run over a dog that has darted into the street may be exponentially more traumatic to the 6-year-old owner of the pet than to the 60-year-old businessman who couldn't stop in time. For me, being gang-raped by three young teenagers one week before my thirtieth birthday, was so traumatic that my brain blocked details of the event for weeks. I only recently discovered through therapy that I had blocked even more details for over 16 years. Pieces of that puzzle are only now starting to come together to a place where I can feel safe about facing my fears. I spent so much time trying to forget about the events of that night. I subconsciously buried the images, smells and sensations deep in the recesses of my mind; not realizing the impact it would have on my whole outlook of life and interaction with others. Issues of trust, fear of the dark and of being alone, and feelings of worthlessness still cloud my better judgment and jump in the pathway of clear thinking.

You may be wondering where my friends and family fit into this scenario. With warped thinking, I felt it was best to hide the events of that night from my family. I only confided in Tom, two close friends, and their two teenage sons. When asked about the bruises on my face, I had a wide variety of lies that, at the time, seemed to settle everyone's curiosity. I even avoided filing a report with the Sheriff's Department for some time. There was, however, the issue of explaining my brief leave-of-absence to the church and school administration. Within two days of the attack, Tom and I went to the pastor of the church with expectations of receiving compassion and Godly counsel on how to move forward after an event that had almost shattered our faith in a good God. To our complete surprise and utter disappointment, I was told not to share this with anyone else – especially the police. If I were to file a report, there would be an investigation and that could certainly cast a bad light on the church administration and parents would begin questioning the safety of their children at school. It must be kept in the smallest circle possible; so as not to spark fear. I was then scolded for being on the property by myself at night.

I pushed the rape deeper and deeper into the shadows of my mind and defaulted back to what had always seemed to work before – busyness. In my naivety I was forcing myself deeper and deeper into the wells of depression and, to make things worse, was working at the "scene of the crime" six days a week; driving the very vehicle I had been assaulted in. Actually, what I was doing was effectively building another wall between me and the ones who loved me the most. At the same time, I was also tearing down the wall between reality and fantasy – these two would soon merge into one shared space in my brain, and instead of living apart from each other they would intertwine and meld into one mass of confusion called 'psychosis'.

> [4] *You are of God, little children, and have overcome them, because He who is in you is greater than he who is in the world.*
>
> *1 John 4:4*

> [6] *Be strong and of good courage, do not fear*
> *nor be afraid of them; for the* LORD *your*
> *God, He is the One who goes with you. He*
> *will not leave you nor forsake you."*

Deuteronomy 31:6

Just The Facts:

- People can live WITH depression - battling it daily; IN depression - surrounded and lonely; UNDER depression – oppressed, in the dark, with no hope; or ABOVE depression – victorious and in control. This much is a choice.

- In the United States, 60% of men and 50% of women experience a traumatic event during their lifetimes. Of those, 8% of men and 20% of women may develop PTSD (Post-Traumatic Stress Disorder). A higher proportion of people who are raped develop PTSD than those who suffer any other traumatic event.[29]

- Some 88% of men and 79% of women with PTSD also have another psychiatric disorder. Nearly half suffer from major depression, 16% from other types of anxiety disorders besides PTSD, and 28% from social phobia. They also are more likely to have risky health behaviors such as alcohol abuse, which affects 52% of men with PTSD and 28% of women, while drug abuse is seen in 35% of men and 27% of women with PTSD.[29]

- In 2007, Behavioral Risk Factor Surveillance System (BRFSS) surveyed adults in 37 states and territories about their attitudes toward mental illness, using the 2007 BRFSS Mental Illness and Stigma module. Based on 2007 BRFSS data,

    1. Most adults with mental health symptoms (78%) and without mental health symptoms (89%) agreed that treatment can help persons with mental illness lead normal lives.
    2. 57% of all adults believed that people are caring and sympathetic to persons with mental illness.
    3. Only 25% of adults with mental health symptoms believed that people are caring and sympathetic to persons with mental illness.

These findings highlight both the need to educate the public about how to support persons with mental illness and the need to reduce barriers for those seeking or receiving treatment for mental illness.[30]

- Depression is the most common type of mental illness, affecting more than 26% of the U.S. adult population.[31] It has been estimated that by the year 2020, depression will be the second leading cause of disability throughout the world, trailing only ischemic heart disease.[32]

A Pastoral Look:

I am not sure if I can ever explain the feelings that a husband goes through when confronted with the sexual assault of his wife. After all, most husbands have a protective instinct and a false sense of swagger that tells the world, "Don't mess with my family or you have to deal with me." You can think that all you want but the simple truth is that you are not omnipresent; you can't be with your family every moment of the day. This world we live in is controlled by Satan, that thief that Jesus warns of in **John 10:10:** ***The thief does not come except to steal, and to kill, and to destroy.*** This very moment threatened to crush Tracy and my views on what life as a believer was supposed to be.

Over the years since the attack happened, I have read several resources on how to deal with such a tragic event. My purpose here is not to repeat those, but rather to give you a personal perspective of what Tracy and I went through - a transparent look into how this horrible event in our life affected what we had already been dealing with. Maybe the best way to start is to share with you the things NOT to do since this is where I unfortunately started. I am incredible ashamed at my complete failure to do what Tracy needed me to do as her husband:

- Do not respond in anger, such uncontrolled anger that you forget that your wife needs you to be in support of her. As a Christian pastor, I have studied extensively the law of non-retaliation Jesus taught in **Matthew 5:38-39**: ***"You have heard that it was said, 'An eye for an eye and a tooth for a tooth' But I tell you not to resist an evil person. But whoever slaps you on your right cheek, turn the other to him also."*** This teaching was not foremost in my mind. While my wife was crying at the kitchen table with her friend, I was getting a gun ready to hunt down these thugs who hurt the woman God had given me to protect. A friend convinced me that murder was never an answer, so I grabbed a baseball bat to go find the offender. I believe the Holy Spirit intervened that night to prevent me from doing something that was against the teachings of my Lord. I am obviously not going to say that a husband is not going to get angry if this were to happen to them, but when that anger turns into wrath and malice, we are in dangerous territory. The scripture tells us that we are to ***"not grieve the Holy Spirit of God, by whom you were sealed for the day of redemption. Let all bitterness, wrath, anger, clamor, and evil speaking be put away from you, with all malice. And be kind to one another, tenderhearted, forgiving one another, even as God in Christ forgave you.*** (Ephesians 4:30-32)** My failure was in not being there emotionally for my wife.

- Do not allow yourself to draw into an emotional shell. When I am overwhelmed, I tend to "stonewall" and avoid showing and even talking about emotions. That is not only unhealthy, but was damaging the love of my life. She NEEDED to connect emotionally, yet I was failing in that way as well. Wasn't I commanded to bear her burden? Of course I was! In fact, I was to do it to "***fulfill the law of Christ.***" (**Galatians 6:2**). Wasn't I supposed to show the same love to her that Christ showed the Church when He gave His life for it according to Ephesians 5? Of course I was! But I was so hurt that I ignored the need Tracy had for me to connect with her on an emotional level. Looking back, I cannot understand how I could have been so obtuse.

- Do not forget to pray for and with your wife. Part of my withdrawal was spiritual. I failed to be the spiritual head of my home because I had built up this impenetrable wall around myself.

- Do not be offended when your wife draws away from your physical touch. She has been traumatized by the unwanted physical abuse of a criminal, and she has to deal with that EVERY DAY. I felt that when Tracy pulled away, she didn't want or need me to touch her. Just the opposite, your wife needs your touch, reassuring her, and reminding her that your touch is used to express deep love and not hurt.

Now those are pretty essential "don'ts" for husbands of women who suffer from the trauma of sexual abuse. Our situation had another element in it that most husbands do not have to consider. Tracy was suffering from severe depression, and this would intensify the situation even more. She was different - not in a bad way, but in the way she was wonderfully made by a sovereign God.

We pastors deal with those who suffer from traumatic events on a regular basis and every situation will be different based upon all the variables (e.g. the emotional and psychological make-up of each individual, the nature of the trauma, the support system the individual has in place). That means that we cannot expect to help and support trauma victims with some sort of cookie cutter approach.

In all the years I have done pastoral counseling I have seen people traumatized by events such as assaults like Tracy's, wartime horrors, accidents, and others too numerous to try to list. The one common thread, whether you are a pastor counseling someone or you are a part of someone's support structure, is this – Christ MUST be at the center of helping the person. In the Living Word are all the answers we need to help someone. I am obviously not saying that the wonderful Christian therapists out there that provide help to the mentally ill are not needed but I am not a psychologist, I am a Christian minister; therefore, I do what God has called me to do. That is to share the truth of the bible – Christ is the source of comfort. That does not mean that He will necessarily remove the effects of our trials and tribulations immediately. He is sovereign and may choose to do so, but often I have seen in my experiences that He chooses to comfort and guide us while we are enduring these situations in order to draw us closer to Him.

I can't stress enough the proper response to trauma victims, especially those suffering from mental illness, as they often process effects of trauma differently from those without these conditions. My choice to react the way I did to the horrific attack on Tracy was *not* a proper response. Looking back at those dark days I realize that I failed to act in a Godly way. I failed to emotionally support my beloved wife who God had commanded me to "love as Christ loved the Church and gave His life for..." (Ephesians 5:25); especially since at the time of the assault I was aware of Tracy's own personal struggles with depression. I think true Christ-like behavior in supporting each other is lacking largely in churches today, especially when it comes to those we deem as "not spiritual enough" because of mental illness. We can talk about how spiritual we are, but as the Holy Spirit inspired James to write, "faith without works is dead." We have to get to the heart of this issue and move past the stigma we have placed upon believers dealing with mental illness. We have to roll up our sleeves and get to work by supporting those God has placed in our lives. I have shared my obviously obtuse actions (and lack of appropriate actions) so you may wonder what my response should have been or what your response should be in a difficult situation like the one Tracy and I were facing. There are many scriptures that reveal the right responses, but I will only share a few examples:

2 Corinthians 1:3-4
***3 Blessed be the God and Father of
our Lord Jesus Christ, the Father
of mercies and God of all comfort,***

***4 who comforts us in all our
tribulation, that we may be able
to comfort those who are in any
trouble, with the comfort with which
we ourselves are comforted by God.***

1 John 3:18
*My little children, let us not
love in word or in tongue,
but in deed and in truth*

Galatians 6:2
*Bear one another's burdens, and
so fulfill the law of Christ...*

On the subject of helping mentally ill Christians, especially those recovering from trauma, I often reflect on the account of the battle against Amalek found in Exodus 17. As long as Moses held up the rod of God, the Israelites would prevail. When his arms dropped, Amalek would have the advantage. Notice what happens in verse 12: ***But Moses' hands became heavy; so they took a stone and put it under him, and he sat on it. And Aaron and Hur supported his hands, one on one side, and the other on the other side; and his hands were steady until the going down of the sun.*** You see, our brothers and sisters in Christ who deal with mental illness often feel like Moses did when his arms grew heavy, with the addition of the characteristics of their condition – tired, despondent, isolated with nowhere to turn, and even suicidal. Our responsibility is not to make light of it nor is it to ignore it. We are to be their Aaron and Hur, supporting them by symbolically keeping their arms lifted during their fight through this often cruel illness. Are you, dear Christian, more like Aaron and Hur, or are you sitting in judgment like Job's "friends?"

Chapter V

DOES THE CHURCH EVEN SEE ME?

A Personal Look:

"Well, it's Sunday again. Time to get ready for church. Sometimes I wonder: what do 'normal' people do on Sunday mornings? I've grown up going to church every Sunday – much like the habit of brushing your teeth every day, or going to work each morning. Today is no different - my hair is not cooperating and it has to be just right or Mrs. Smith will offer her hairdresser's name and number to me again. Does this skirt touch my knees at the proper place? If it's too short, I will hear about it from Ms. Thomas. I must be careful that I wear a slip, and that it doesn't show beneath the hemline of my skirt. My make-up needs to be complimentary to my natural features – too little and I look sickly; too much and I look like a "working girl". At least that's what Mrs. Carlton says. My top can't be too revealing and absolutely must have sleeves. Some modest jewelry is appropriate, but not so much as to draw attention to myself. Why do I worry so much about what people think anyway? Sometimes I wish I wasn't a Pastor's wife. That whole saying about living in a fishbowl is so true! People are unbelievably bold when it comes to judging the family of the one called to serve them. I heard once that the Pastor is like unto the shepherds of years past. If that's true, I think every "shepherd's wife" needs to be warned that the sheep BITE! This level of anxiety certainly can't be good for me; but it's only for a few hours, then I can relax a little and take off my plastic smile."

Natalie Grant captures the heart of where I am with the lyrics to her song, *The Real Me.*

> *Foolish heart, looks like we're here again*
> *Same old game of plastic smile*
> *Don't let anybody in*
> *Hiding my heartache, will*
> *this glass house break*
> *How much will they take*
> *before I'm empty*
> *Do I let it show, does anybody know*

CHORUS:

But You see the real me
Hiding in my skin, broken from within
Unveil me completely
I'm loosening my grasp
There's no need to mask my frailty
Cause You see the real me

Painted on, life is behind a mask
Self-inflicted circus clown
I'm tired of the song and dance
Living a charade, always on parade
What a mess I've made of my existence
But You love me even now
And still I see somehow

But You see the real me
Hiding in my skin, broken from within
Unveil me completely
I'm loosening my grasp
There's no need to mask my frailty
Cause You see the real me

Wonderful, beautiful is what You see
When You look at me
You're turning the tattered
fabric of my life into
A perfect tapestry
I just wanna be me

But You see the real me
Hiding in my skin, broken from within
Unveil me completely
I'm loosening my grasp
There's no need to mask my frailty
Cause You see the real me

And You love me just as I am
Wonderful, beautiful is what You see
When You look at me.

"There's no way I can measure up to what everyone wants me to be. I'm not the perfect wife. I'm not the perfect mother. I'm certainly not the perfect Christian! But neither are they, so why am I being lifted up on this public pedestal, being put against a list of standards I can never live up to? I should be able to just ignore the critical spirit of the few, and be assured by the tender speech of the rest; but it's never that easy. If this is the church, do I really want to be a part of it? Then again, how could I NOT be a part of it? This is the family of God! It would be so much easier for me to pull into myself and just listen to the voice of my Savior from the comfort of my own home. Even better, I can retreat to my castle. It's safe and quiet there. [*Do you see how easily I slid right into dissociative thinking?*] No one comes in the castle gates without my invitation. In fact, very few have ever been there. I bring my Rottweiler, Sophie, with me and there are two beautiful horses in the stable – one paint and one sorrel. There's a wonderful meadow beyond the west wall with plenty of clover and wildflowers to run through. The surrounding forest is friendly and inviting, offering shade when I am overcome by the heat of the summer day. The creek always has pure, cold, refreshing water tripping over the smooth stones of the creek bed. I can always hear the breeze whispering in the tree-tops as I lift my face to the sun. If only I could stay here. It's always a comforting, forgiving and safe place for me to come when things are ugly and painful in the real world."

Over time, the stress of life would become too much for my fragile mind to handle and I attempted to leave this life by slitting my left wrist. I simply wanted all the pain and frustration to leave my body in the flow of red blood down my fingertips. I don't remember a lot about the incident, other than a bad mix of medications sent me into a suicidal tailspin and my best friend found me in the bathroom of the church and took me to the hospital. I spent the next 6 days in a behavioral health facility under observation. It was a horribly "non-Christian" experience that I never want to repeat! It did, however, get me focused back on taking care of myself and not letting the opinions of others so rule my life that it threatened my well-being. After a full month off of work, a handful of new prescriptions, and a myriad of doctor and psychiatric appointments, I was back on my feet and trying life again. With a flurry of questions and suspicions floating through the church, Tom and I felt it best if I addressed the congregation with a straight-forward explanation of what had happened. I stood on a Sunday morning in front of a wide variety of faces and tried my best to explain my diagnosis of "severe depression" with a brief explanation of my hospital stay. My goal was to be genuine, transparent, and available; without disclosing too many personal details. The response I got was mixed. I was surprised at how many people comforted me through their own tears of silent suffering and applauded me on my bravery. Then there were those who slipped out the back door, not wanting to face me...not knowing what to say, now that they knew... and who conveniently never spoke with me again. Later accusations of me "not being friendly" to them seemed to cover their ignorant fear of my "label". Had the pastor not been my husband, I wonder if I would have stopped going to church. The humiliation following my testimony and the invisibility of my illness could have easily kept me outside the church's doors instead of inside the safety of the fellowship of believers. Mental illness carries a horrible stigma within the ranks of God's people and we have to do something about it! Understandably so, the mentally ill are a hard group of people to reach. Sometimes their symptoms and side effects of medications seem to stand in the way of a comfortable conversation. We misinterpret their behaviors to mean they are self-absorbed, lazy, or failing to trust God. We distance ourselves, ignoring them, rejecting them, or fearing them, ultimately shaming them back into silence. A better response might be to recognize something of yourself in the other person and nurture a connection, resisting the urge to minimalize or demonize their situation. Acknowledge any superstitious beliefs about mental illness and replace those thoughts with the visualization of how Christ would treat that person. None of us can offer all the answers, but all of us can certainly offer a smile and extend dignity to a fellow child of the King.

> [3] *For though we walk in the flesh, we do not war according to the flesh.* [4] *For the weapons of our warfare are not carnal but mighty in God for pulling down strongholds,* [5] *casting down arguments and every high thing that exalts itself against the knowledge of God, bringing every thought into captivity to the obedience of Christ,*
>
> *2 Corinthians 10:3-5*

> *He shall cover you with His feathers, And under His wings you shall take refuge; His truth shall be your shield and buckler.*
>
> *Psalm 91:4*

Just The Facts:

- We know from a recent study that nearly as many troubled people seek counseling from clergymen as from all other helping professions combined.[33]

- Researchers surveyed nearly 6,000 participants in 24 churches representing four Protestant denominations about their family's stresses, strengths, faith practices and desires for assistance from the congregation. The results showed mental illness in **27 percent** of families, with those families reporting **double** the number of stressors, such as financial strain and problems balancing work and family. Families with mental illness also scored lower on measures of family strength and faith practices, and analysis of desires for assistance found that help with mental illness was a priority for those families affected by it, but **virtually ignored** by others in the congregation.[34]

- A study found that approximately one-third of the study's participants diagnosed with a mental disorder reported having a negative experience with a church when they sought help for a mental health issue.[35]

- Quote by Gunnar Christiansen, M.D., presented at the 2003 NAMI Oregon Convention: "Spiritual strength will diminish, however, unless it is constantly nurtured through giving and receiving loving care in our relationships with others. Thus it is of major importance that each of us attempts to develop a welcome and spiritually nourishing environment for those affected by mental illness in our own place of worship."

- More than 90 percent of people who kill themselves have a diagnosable mental disorder.[36]

- The significance of one's faith has shown to lower one's risk of depressive symptoms and aid one in better handling a stressful medical event.[37]

A Pastoral Look:

Tracy desired with all her heart to worship like others, without feelings of worthlessness. Even though these same leaders would have no problem helping others that were dealing with feelings of shame and hopelessness due to "regular illnesses" and chronic conditions; they would not do so with Tracy. Did they really think that she could just wave a wand and make it all go away? Was the consensus therefore that mental illness is not "real"? The answers we found were staggering. The many Christians suffering from mental illness were unable to find help from where they desired to seek it the most - their church, the Body of Christ. I watched Tracy's walls grow bigger and stronger as she strived to put on a "church face" and pretend that nothing was wrong. Her identity began to be more focused on what she was enduring.

Our identity as Christians is not based on what works we have done, or even in the successes and failures of our relationships. What would you answer if I asked you simply, "Who are you?" Unfortunately, some may answer that they are a mom, dad, engineer, teacher, landscaper, or wife. Think about how many times you meet someone for the very first time and the inevitable question surfaces: "What do you do?" Even in the ministry, when I meet fellow pastors, we often ask each other about where we went to seminary or how many our church runs. Society has taught us that these types of things define who we are. Even our private thoughts of who we are can be dictated by these boundaries. This is where Tracy was - secretly feeling her identity was inseparable from her illness yet outwardly acting as if her identity was as a pastor's wife, mother, counselor to everyone else in need. This is a recipe for disaster, and as we would find out, it was just a matter of time before Tracy would crumble beneath the weight of it all without the help of her church and family. Brothers and sisters in Christ let me remind you that your identity is not determined by any of these previously mentioned things but rather by your relationship with God. I am a pastor, dad, papa, and husband; but I am not wrapped up in the identity of those things. My identity is that of a blood-washed child of the King, ordained unto good works and given life, and life more abundantly!

I do not want anyone to mistake this as a typical "Christian" response akin to "Well, if you will just realize you are Christ's, the mental health issues will just go away. You just need more faith!" What we have to understand is yes, our identity is in Christ, but our struggles and trials in this sin-cursed body are very diverse and of differing degrees of seriousness. I know of a pastor who was diagnosed with ALS (sometimes referred to as Lou Gehrig's Disease). He spent his adult life investing in many lives through ministry. A fabulous preacher, a loving pastor, a family man, a man of character, an unashamed witness – these are a few characteristics of who he is; however, they are *not* his identity. Having ALS does not identify *who* he is. This obedient servant of Christ's identity is as a child of God. The ALS is a *trial* God allowed for him to endure for reasons we will probably never know. Instead of us looking at him as "that poor man who has ALS," we should instead see him first and foremost as a Christian who happens to have ALS. I want to see the Body of Christ, believers everywhere, to rally around our brothers and sisters that suffer from mental illness and let them know we see them as Christians primarily. THAT is their identity! Next, do not ignore their mental illness but become an integral part of their support system; not sitting in judgment, giving uninformed advice, or ignoring the issue at hand, but truly embracing them and taking this journey beside them.

> *"Therefore, if anyone is in Christ, he is a new creation; old things have passed away; behold, all things have become new."*
>
> 2 Corinthians 5:17

> *"giving thanks to the Father who has qualified us to be partakers of the inheritance of the saints in the light"*
>
> Colossians 1:12

Chapter VI

WHAT DO PASTORS
NEED TO KNOW?

A Personal Look:

"It's sure beautiful here by the gate. I can see for miles down through the valley. The rose bushes are blooming nicely and their sweet aroma fills the air as I stroll by. Maybe I'll invite a friend in to go for a ride this afternoon. The horses can take us up past the meadow and into the woods where I can check on the fox and her new kits. I love spring-time at the castle! I know my closest friends and my therapist are not fond of me traveling to the castle, because they're afraid one of these days I won't come home. I go over in my mind what that would be like. Would it really be that bad to stay here where things are peaceful and simple? Don't I deserve that? After all, I have had more than my share of hardship and trouble;

sickness and pain. I've lost 2 babies, Alex and Bethany, to miscarriage. Two of my four children struggle with depression, like me. My father is slowly succumbing to dementia. My husband is burdened with more than his share of ailments: diabetes, epilepsy, neuropathy, and kidney failure, to name a few. I've lost a good friend and mother-in-law to cancer and my precious grandmother has gone on to heaven's shores as well. I've survived a near-fatal car accident and subsequent back surgery. I'm a rape survivor. Church people – fellow Christians – have back-stabbed, gossiped, and downright lied in an attempt to push us out of ministry. My testimony is bruised and battered, aching for relief from the torments of those within the Christian ranks. I should be allowed to sit down beside the stream and just concentrate on the sound of the water tripping over the smooth stones. I should be able to breathe in the scent of fresh hay in the barn as the horses eat their breakfast. All the troubles of this life should jump up on the shelf and wait while I lay in the grassy meadow and feel the gentle breeze blow through my hair. No tears, no pain, just kisses from my Rottweiler and….. wait…. This isn't reality. Or is it a reality that no one but me can experience? Does anyone else see my castle and all it holds? Surely the guardian must see all that I see. What about my prince? I need help!"

It's difficult to accept that sometimes what I see and what I hear is not real. In MY mind, it's VERY real!

Those who struggle with mental illness fight invisible battles that some won't understand and it affects their spiritual life in ways that are nearly impossible to explain.

If I had the top 100 most influential pastors in America all in one room and was given 15 minutes to tell them what the most important things to know about my mental illness are, I would tell them this:

1. My mental illness holds the same weight as a physical illness when asking God for healing.

If John Pew-warmer came to you and the elders with a cast on his leg, asking you to pray over him for healing, (as instructed in James 5:14), you would in no wise turn him away. Treat me the same way. Just because my illness is not visible to the eye does not mean it doesn't exist.

2. Don't be afraid of me, be informed.

Please don't assume that I am demonically possessed or unrepentant of sin. As with any other member of your congregation that is having problems, that very well could be the case, but please don't automatically jump to that conclusion. Take the time to sit down with me and treat me the way you would address someone who was just diagnosed with cancer.

I'm hurting, confused, and need your spiritual guidance.

3. **Know your limitations in a counseling setting and don't be afraid to refer me to a mental health professional.**

Just as you would not call on a plumber to examine your cat, don't rely on your spiritual knowledge and expertise to effectively help what may be a medical condition. After your professional assessment of the situation, if the problem goes beyond your level of counseling ability, please defer to a therapist, psychologist, or psychiatrist that can help. Sometimes something as simple as properly prescribed medication can be a life-saving answer. Here is a list of "red flags" that might signal the need for follow-up with a medical doctor or psychiatric professional: [1]

In adults:

- Confused thinking
- Prolonged depression (sadness or irritability)
- Feelings of extreme highs and lows
- Excessive fears, worries and anxieties
- Social withdrawal

- Dramatic changes in eating or sleeping habits
- Strong feelings of anger
- Delusions or hallucinations
- Growing inability to cope with daily problems and activities
- Suicidal thoughts
- Denial of obvious problems
- Numerous unexplained physical ailments
- Substance abuse

In older children and pre-adolescents:

- Substance abuse
- Inability to cope with problems and daily activities
- Changes in sleeping and/or eating habits
- Excessive complaints of physical ailments
- Defiance of authority, truancy, theft, and/or vandalism
- Intense fear of weight gain
- Prolonged negative mood, often accompanied by poor appetite or thoughts of death
- Frequent outbursts of anger

In younger children:

- Changes in school performance
- Poor grades despite strong efforts
- Excessive worry or anxiety (i.e. refusing to go to bed or school)
- Hyperactivity
- Persistent nightmares
- Persistent disobedience or aggression
- Frequent temper tantrums

4. **I need to know I still have worth in the Kingdom. Help me find a place to serve and stay engaged in the life of the congregation.**

Just because I have depression does not mean that I am a danger to children. Just because I've been diagnosed with bi-polar disorder does not mean that I can't greet people at the door, or sing in the choir, or collect the offering. Don't misunderstand - necessary precautions should always be taken to protect your flock from dangerous people; but instead of jumping to that conclusion, help me find something… anything to do to serve my Savior. Allowing and encouraging me to get involved in ministry actually helps my condition!

5. **Give me reassurance that I am welcome and that you are willing to pray me through this difficult journey.**

All of us have strengths and all of us have challenges. I'm just asking for the chance to use my strengths, despite my challenge, to bless the hearts of God's people. My deepest desire is to bring glory to His name and further His kingdom!

────ᘏᘏᘏᘏᘏ────

[10] Create in me a clean heart, O God, And renew a steadfast spirit within me. [12] Restore to me the joy of Your salvation, And uphold me by Your generous Spirit. [15] O Lord, open my lips, And my mouth shall show forth Your praise. [16] For You do not desire sacrifice, or else I would give it; You do not delight in burnt offering. [17] The sacrifices of God are a broken spirit, A broken and a contrite heart – These, O God, You will not despise.

Psalm 51: 10, 12, 15 - 17

Just The Facts:

- 67.6% of respondents in this study cited religion and spirituality as playing a role in helping their family care for a mentally ill member, making it one of the most frequently cited resilience factors.[38]

- "Patients are often distressed by the effect that the mental illness has on their ability to practice and express their faith."[39]

- "Clergy tend to be sought out first and at greater rates than mental health professionals by individuals concerned about their functioning."[39]

- "Religious leaders can better serve these families by building relationships with local mental health providers and learning what resources are available outside the congregation. As their knowledge and resource base expands, they can respond more effectively to those who seek their counsel. At the same time, they can help mental health providers understand religious beliefs, values and practices that can be resources for clients and their families."[39]

A Pastoral Look:

Growing up, like a lot of kids, I was terrified of imaginary monsters and creatures that I was sure lurked under my bed, in my closet, and in the shadowy corners of my room. My older brothers taught me that the only defense against sure death at the hands (or claws) of these horrors was to pull my blankets up over my head tightly. That's right, if you cannot see the monster, then he cannot get you! When the local church ignores the pleas for help from the mentally ill in their congregations, they are hoping that by "pulling their covers up over their heads" they will keep the specter of depression and other disease from affecting them. The end result is that Christians are going elsewhere for help, and are being inundated by worldly views of psychology and "cures" for their condition. Unfortunately, this will leave a believer in a precarious position of allowing their minds to be conformed to this world. This wisdom of man is made "foolish" by God (1 Corinthians 1:20). Thankfully, God has some wonderful, productive verses about dealing with depression.

> *"Why are you cast down, O my soul? And why are you disquieted within me? Hope in God, for I shall yet praise Him For the help of His countenance. …For You are the God of my strength…"*

> *Psalm 42:5, 43:2*

I have observed while pastoring that ignoring a real problem in the church is never the right response. It is almost like allowing a malignant tumor to remain without treatment with the hope it will go away on its own. Without any intervention, be it medical or God, that tumor will continue to grow. It will grow by attacking healthy cells around it until destruction becomes more and more inevitable. Church problems are the same way. When they are ignored they begin to spread throughout the congregation. This is what leads to much of the ignorance and fear of mental illness within the Body of Christ. We need to face the reality of the very real struggle it is causing amidst our congregations.

Many pastors and Christian lay leaders have taken a very dangerous "hands-off" approach to the members of our congregations when it comes to mental illness, situational depression, and emotional needs. I actually had a pastor of a large church tell me, "I will not do any sort of counseling." Surely I must have misheard him! I responded to him, "Well I realize that we as pastors have our limitations…." He then replied, "It causes more problems than it is worth so I just started telling people to find counseling somewhere else." He even went so far as to refuse to allow any of his staff (some very qualified) to do any counseling. That meant no offer of scriptural comfort and assurance from God for the mentally ill; no giving of necessary tools to an engaged couple to promote a Godly marriage; no counseling to help a husband and wife with a marriage crisis; no sitting down with a family that needed to learn about what the Bible says regarding communication – not these or any of the multiple ministry counseling opportunities we have that invests in lives.

In our research for this book we found a poll that speaks about how most churches and most pastors do not believe that mental illness is real. Unfortunately, from my personal standpoint, I have discovered that these polls hit the nail on the head. When I have spoken to my peers about mental illness I have seen their countenance change – they simply do not want to deal with the subject. Is it an illness with a physical or biological basis? Is it demonic possession or oppression? Is it something that people have to "get over?" I would rather have preachers at least join in intellectual exchange of information than to ignore the reality of mental illness. I am very convicted that we are at a place in the Church's history that if we simply brush off the issue, we will see the ignorance of leadership and the pain and isolation of the afflicted in the pews cause a schism that will cause significant damage within the Body of Christ. This schism, if we continue this course, will significantly affect our ability to evangelize a world which desperately needs Christ. How can we reach the world for Christ if we allow our own brothers and sisters in faith to hurt while we idly stand by?

> *12 Therefore, as the elect of God, holy and beloved, put on tender mercies, kindness, humility, meekness, longsuffering;*
>
> *Colossians 3:12*

18 My little children, let us not love in word or in tongue, but in deed and in truth.

1 John 3:18

Chapter VII

WILL YOU MAKE A DIFFERENCE?

A Personal Look:

"I just need you to let me know what's happening! I don't know where I am or why I can only be on the phone for 5 minutes or less. It's very scary in this place. I want to go home! What did I do to get myself in here? What day is it? When are you coming to get me?"

I would soon learn that I had been admitted to the local behavioral health hospital. I had been there two days and was just now coherent enough to realize my situation. Fact: I had taken far too many of a particular anti-psychotic medication and was being treated for an over-dose. Within the past few months I had experienced several traumatic life changes and was not handling them in stride. My daughter had just gotten married, we recently resigned from a church to start a new ministry, Tom's health had taken a turn for the worse, and my best friends were suddenly taking a less prominent role in my day to day life. For me, these things were in sum, devastating. I was spending many of my evenings at the castle, finding reality much too difficult to bear. As the boundary lines between here and psychosis started to blur, my struggle to maintain clarity was slowly caving in and I finally succumbed to the relief of over-medication. It would be many more days before I could think clearly. It was in this critical, fragile time that the people who knew me best would be strength and comfort to me. And in those times when they were not allowed to be by my side, the Lord reminded me who I was in Him. His sweet whispers of truth and peace would calm my restless spirit. I found music to be a particular treasure during these dark days; but when I had no song, the Lord sang a sweet and comforting lullaby over my soul that lulled me back into His light. You see, many things will help the broken mind – friends, family, music, pets – but none like the constant and true voice of the Savior. He melts the madness that can so swiftly overtake my feeble thoughts, as so beautifully arranged in the song, *You Melt the Madness,* by Jericho Road.

So when you ask what you can do or what you can say to someone you know experiences mental complications, there's no easy answer. Encourage them to find what works for them and then offer to be a part of their support team to keep these things that work in the forefront of their lives on those dismal days when life attacks with its full fury. Some days I need to curl up with my sweet Rottweiler, Sophie, and take a long nap. Some days just plugging my i-pod in and listening to my "healing" playlist will pull me up. Other days I need my friends and family walking every step with me to make sure I survive 'til the next hour. Mental illness is not a pretty malady, but it is a survivable one when reliance is placed on the Lord and all the comforts He provides in their many forms and fashions.

> [9]*Have I not commanded you? Be strong and of good courage; do not be afraid, nor be dismayed, for the Lord your God is with you wherever you go.*
>
> *Joshua 1:9*

> [10] *Fear not, for I am with you; Be not dismayed, for I am your God. I will strengthen you, Yes, I will help you. I will uphold you with My righteous right hand.*
>
> *Isaiah 41:10*

Just The Facts:

- The weight of evidence, on average and across studies, suggests that religion, however assessed, is a generally protective factor for mental illness.[40]

- People in creative professions are treated more often for mental illness than the general population.[41]

- Recent research has uncovered findings which suggest that to some patients religion may also be a resource that helps them to cope with the stress of their illness or with dismal life circumstances.[42]

- Study: People Who Believe in God Are More Responsive to Treatment of Depression[43]

A Pastoral Look:

After reading this book I pray that you realize the importance of knowing the reality of certain things: mental illness is a real disease; demonic possession is an undeniable segment of spiritual warfare that may share symptoms of mental illness; Christians, however, cannot be possessed by demonic forces because God the Holy Spirit dwells within us; and we as the Body of Christ must not dismiss mental illness or ignore it.

I truly believe that the Word of God is inerrant, infallible, and inspired. I believe with all that I am that contained in the pages of the Holy Writ are all the answers we need for living life with Christ in us. Period. This does not mean that we can pick up the Bible and be able to always understand "why." Why did the holocaust occur under the direction of Adolph Hitler? What about the lives taken by Joseph Stalin, Mao Tse Tung, Saddam Hussein, and all of the other despots throughout the history of the world? I recently did a funeral for a precious 3 month old baby girl. With all the evil in the world, was I able to look the family in their eyes and tell them why it was their baby? Absolutely not. And to my fellow pastors – clichés and assailing them with verses is not what a family in grieving needs. They need one or two verses of assurance and then let them know the most important truth. You cannot explain why, but you love them and God loves them. Let them know God is for them. Let them know you are there for whatever they need, even if that means just sitting there and letting them mourn. I am not sure I will ever understand most of the "why" part of life. The prophet Isaiah declared this concept in **Isaiah 55:9** *"For as the heavens are higher than the earth, So are My ways higher than your ways, And My thoughts than your thoughts."* Sometimes He will reveal why things happen and sometimes He does not. This, my dear friends, is where faith comes in. Instead of blaming God, getting angry at Him, or turning your back to Him you must realize that it is *by faith* that we are commanded to live. When I struggle, such as when that young baby died, I run to the same passage in the bible – **Romans 8:28** *"And we know that <u>all things work together for good</u> to those who love God, to those who are the called according to His purpose."* We do not need to know why – it is for us to be obedient bond-servants of Christ that know by faith that everything happens for a reason. God is not scrambling to react to us, He is in control. Paul reassures the Philippians in **chapter 2 verse 13**, *"for it is God who works in you both to will and to do for His good pleasure."*

It is in this same way we must deal with true mental illness. Tracy has struggled with her clinical depression by going to God many times in prayer. With complete transparency and honesty she has let her cries be known to our God. He has chosen, at least for now, to not answer her prayers for healing (we will continually pray for that healing). It therefore becomes a faith issue for her. There are no perfect or super Christians out there. I know some pastors that need to be reminded of the words of Paul, *"This is a faithful saying and worthy of all acceptance, that Christ Jesus came into the world to save sinners, <u>of whom I am chief</u>."* **(I Timothy 1:15)** When Tracy went to several church leaders over the years about her life-long battle with depression she was cast aside by the very people she thought could help her most. When a mentally ill Christian is simply told they need to just "have more faith" or "you have nothing to be depressed about" it deflates them and makes them feel worthless. As far as Tracy, she felt diminished by these pastors and other leaders. Tracy shared with me that the impression she got from all of these types of answers is that she could not match up to other Christians and she was disappointing church leadership and God.

Beloved pastors and other church leaders, let us remember why we are in the ministry. God has called us to literally be <u>servants</u> to the people in the Body of Christ. Look with me at **I Timothy 4:6** ***"If you instruct the brethren in these things, <u>you will be a good minister of Jesus Christ</u>, nourished in the words of faith and of the good doctrine which you have carefully followed."*** The word "minister" is from the Greek word *diakonos*, literally translated as "one who executes the commands of another." God commands us to serve one another; therefore we are to execute this command within the Body of Christ. Thayer also gives us another definition I like for this same Greek word, "one who does what promotes the welfare and prosperity of the church." My friends, are we promoting the welfare of the church when we ignore or make the plight of mentally ill Christians problematic? Of course we aren't – we are falling short of what God desires for us as ministers to do for His glory. If we do not love the mentally ill, embrace them with the love of Christ, pray with and for them, counsel them through God's Word, and reinforce their place and worth in the ministry then we are failing to follow what God has called us to do. Tracy deals with severe clinical depression and had a short period of psychoses. Yet she is a classically trained pianist, a singer, a teacher, and wonderful at organizing VBS and other church events. She has been gifted by the Holy Spirit to serve others. If some pastors out there would have their way by ignoring her or making her feel useless, they would miss out on what God called her to do in service to the King. I have been privileged to be Tracy's pastor now for some time and I cannot imagine church without her beautiful smile, contagious service, and desire to see souls redeemed through what Christ has done.

How many "Tracys" do you have in your church? How are you ministering to them and are you treating them in a way that facilitates "promoting the welfare of the church"? The mentally ill are out there. They are in our pews. They are in Sunday School rooms. They are in the nursery. They are in choir lofts and maybe in our pulpits. They are looking for answers, and if the church cannot provide the love and support they need, they will look elsewhere. We will then run the danger of them being exposed to ungodly and dangerous treatment and information. What will you do? Will you rise to the challenge or be apathetic to the need of these mentally ill people that are loved so much by God? Dear pastor, we have a choice to make. What will you do?

Closing Statement:

Our prayer is that the information we have just put in your hands will cause you to take a moment to ask the Lord if your response to the mental illness community is one that brings glory to the Father. Is there someone you know that you have ignored because of not knowing how to respond to what seems to be a mental health problem? Has the word of our testimony caused you to re-evaluate your relationships? If you still have questions, please seek help! We highly recommend the counseling line at *Focus on the Family* as a good start. They can recommend counselors in your area or further resources to expand your knowledge on this topic. We have also included a resource page of websites, books, music and organizations that have helped us on our journey and will certainly bring further light to yours. Thank you for being open to this tender chapter of our lives and as John 10:10 proclaims: may you have life more abundantly!

> *"The thief does not come except to steal, and to kill, and to destroy. I have come that they may have life, and that they may have it **more abundantly**."*

LIST OF RESOURCES

WEBSITES:

- www.psyweb.com
- www.nami.org
- www.webmd.com/mental-health
- www.nmha.org
- www.psychiatry.org/mental-health/
- www.nimh.nih.gov

MUSIC:

- Trust His Heart by Babbie Mason
- Enough by BarlowGirl
- It's Alright by Brandon Heath
- Jesus, Hold Me Now by Casting Crowns
- Broken Into Beautiful; Uncluttered; & Healer of the Broken by Gwen Smith
- Angel By Your Side by Francesca Battistelli
- Lay It Down by Jaci Velasquez
- Lift Me Up; Come To Jesus; You Melt the Madness; & If I Lost My Way by Jericho Road

- Fall Apart & They Just Believe by Josh Wilson
- A Love That Won't Walk Away & He Will Shelter You by Kathy Troccoli
- Take You Away & Keep Breathing by Kerrie Roberts
- Blessings by Laura Story
- Broken Hallelujah & He Will Come by Mandisa
- Hello, My Name Is by Matthew West
- The Hurt and The Healer & Keep Singing by Mercy Me
- Can Anybody Hear Me; You're Not Alone & Show Me What It Means by Meredith Andrews
- The Real Me; I Am Not Alone; At Your Feet; Our Hope Endures by Natalie Grant
- Need You Now by Plumb
- Not Alone by Red
- I Turn To You; Hold On & Press On by Selah
- Let Go by Sheila Walsh
- Arms That Hold The Universe by 33Miles

BOOKS:

- Grace For the Afflicted…a Clinical and Biblical Perspective on Mental Illness by Matthew S. Stanford, PhD, Paternoster Publishing 2008
- When Your Family Is Living With Mental Illness by Marcia Lund, Augsburg Books 2002

- Conquering Depression – a 30-day Plan to Finding Happiness by Mark Sutton & Bruce Hennigan, M.D., B&H Publishing Group 2001
- Breaking Through Depression by Donald P. Hall, M.D., Harvest House Publishers 2009
- Honestly by Sheila Walsh, Zondervan 1996
- New Light On Depression by David B. Biebel, D.Min. & Harold G. Koenig, M.D., Zondervan 2004
- The Freedom From Depression Workbook by Les Carter, Ph.D. & Frank Minirth, M.D., Thomas Nelson 1995
- Lincoln's Melancholy by Joshua Wolf Shenk, Mariner Books 2005
- Breaking Free From Depression by Linda Mintle, Ph.D., Charisma House 2002
- Breaking Through Depression by Donald P. Hall, M.D., Harvert House Publishers 2009
- First Aid For Your Emotional Hurts – Depression by Edward E. Moody, Jr., Ph.D., Randall House 2010

ENDNOTES

1. Edward B. Rodgers, Matthew Stanford & Diana R. Garland (2012): The effects of mental illness on families within faith communities, Mental Health, Religion & Culture, 15:3, 301-313

2. Study published in *Psychiatric Services*, April 2004. Reported our health news archive: Pill-Popping Pre-Schoolers, Even Toddlers Get the Blues.

3. Irina V. Sokolova at the Rochester Institute of Technology http://www.childhooddepression.us/articles6.html.

4. AACAP (American Academy of Child and Adolescent Psychiatry).

5. http://holistichealthlibrary.com/depression-and-anxiety-on-the-rise/

6. http://www.depression-test.net/depression-statistics.html

7. http://www.sciencedirect.com/science/article/pii/S0022395612002804

8. When Your Family Is Living With Mental Illness by Marcia Lund – Augsburg Books, 2002

9. Grace For the Afflicted; a Clinical and Biblical Perspective on Mental Illness by Matthew S Stanford, PhD; Paternoster Publishing, 2008

10. Grace For the Afflicted; a Clinical and Biblical Perspective on Mental Illness by Matthew S Stanford, PhD; Paternoster Publishing, 2008

11 U.S. Select Committee on Children, Youth & Families, www.nami.org

12 www.nami.org

13 http://www.nami.org/PrinterTemplate.cfm?Section=Sample_Letter_to_Clergy&site=FaithNet

14 U.S. Department of Health and Human Services. *Mental Health: A Report of the Surgeon General.* Rockville,MD: U.S. Department of Health and Human Services, Substance Abuse and Mental Health Services Administration, Center for Mental Health Services, National Institutes of Health, National Institute of Mental Health, 1999.

15. New Freedom Commission on Mental Health, *Achieving the Promise: Transforming Mental Health Care in America. Final Report.* DHHS Pub. No. SMA-0303832. Rockville, MD: 2003.

16 National Institute of Mental Health Release of landmark and collaborative study conducted by Harvard University, the University of Michigan and the NIMH Intramural Research Program (release dated June 6, 2005 and accessed at www.nimh.nih.gov).

17 American Psychological Association (APA): mental illness. (n.d.). *The American Heritage Stedman's Medical Dictionary.* Retrieved April 12, 2012, from dictionary.com website: http://dictionary.reference.com/browse/mentalillness

18 'When Your Family Is Living With Mental Illness' by Marcia Lund, Augsburg Books 2002

19 http://www.mayoclinic.com/health/mental-illness/DS01104/DSECTION=symptoms

20 http://www.psychiatry.org/mental-health/more-topics/warning-signs-of-mental-illness

21 http://abcnews.go.com/blogs/health/2012/01/19/1-in-5-americans-suffer-from-mental-illness/

22 http://science.education.nih.gov/supplements/nih5/mental/guide/info-mental-a.htm

23 Kessler RC, Chiu WT, Demler O, Walters EE. Prevalence, severity, and comorbidity of twelve-month DSM-IV disorders

in the National Comorbidity Survey Replication (NCS-R). *Archives of General Psychiatry*, 2005 Jun;62(6):617-27.

[24] Grace For the Afflicted by Matthew S. Stanford, PhD pg. 119

[25] The World Health Organization. *The global burden of disease: 2004 update*, Table A2: Burden of disease in DALYs by cause, sex and income group in WHO regions, estimates for 2004. Geneva, Switzerland: WHO, 2008. http://www.who.int/healthinfo/global_burden_disease/GBD_report_2004update_AnnexA.pdf.

[26] http://www.health.com/health/gallery/0,20393228_11,00.html

[27] http://science.education.nih.gov/supplements/nih5/mental/guide/info-mental-a.htm

[28] http://science.education.nih.gov/supplements/nih5/mental/guide/info-mental-a.htm

[29] http://www.webmd.com/mental-health/post-traumatic-stress-disorder-ptsd

[30] http://www.cdc.gov/mmwr/preview/mmwrhtml/mm5920a3.htm

[31] Kessler RC, Chiu WT, Demler O, Walters EE. Prevalence, severity, and comorbidity of 12-month DSM-IV disorders in the National Comorbidity Survey Replication. *Arch Gen Psychiatry* 2005;62:617–627.

[32] Murray CJL, Lopez AD. *The Global Burden of Disease: A Comprehensive Assessment of Mortality and Disability from Diseases, Injuries and Risk Factors in 1990 and Projected to 2020.* Geneva, Switzerland;World Health Organization, 1996.

[33] Gerald Gurin, et al., Americans View Their Mental Health (New York: Basic Books, Inc., 1960), p. 307.

[34] Baylor University (2011, June 22). Church congregations can be blind to mental illness, study suggests. *ScienceDaily.* Retrieved April 12, 2013, from http://www.sciencedaily.com / releases/2011/06/110622115307.htm

[35] Stanford, M. S. (2007). Demon or Disorder: A Survey of Attitudes Toward Mental Illness in the Christian Church. *Mental Health, Religion & Culture, 10*(5), 445-449.

[36] Conwell Y, Brent D. Suicide and aging I: patterns of psychiatric diagnosis. International Psychogeriatrics, 1995; 7(2): 149-64.

37 Pressman P., Lyons J.S., Larson D.B., Strain, J.J. "Religious belief, depression, and ambulation status in elderly women with broken hips." American Journal of Psychiatry 1990; 147(6): 758-760.

38 http://www.nmha.org/go/information/get-info/mi-and-the-family/recognizing-warning-signs-and-how-to-cope

39 Edward B. Rodgers, Matthew Stanford & Diana R. Garland (2012): The effects of mental illness on families within faith communities, Mental Health, Religion & Culture, 15:3, 301-313

40 Religion and Mental Health:Theory and Research, International Journal of Applied Psychoanalytic Studies, *Int. J. Appl. Psychoanal. Studies* (2010), Published online in Wiley InterScience, (www.interscience.wiley.com) **DOI**: 10.1002/aps.240

41 Karolinska Institutet. "Link between creativity and mental illness confirmed in large-scale Swedish study." *ScienceDaily*, 16 Oct. 2012.

42 The Psychiatrist (2008) 32: 201-203 doi: 10.1192/pb.bp.108.019430

43 http://www.theatlantic.com/health/archive/2013/04/study-people-who-believe-in-god-are-more-responsive-to-treatment-of-depression/275314/